First Facts®

Long Ago and Today

TRANSPORTATION

LONG AGO and TODAY

by Lisa M. Bolt Simons

Consultant:
Daniel Zielske
Professor of Anthropology
South Central College
North Mankato, Minnesota

CAPSTONE PRESS
a capstone imprint

First Facts are published by Capstone Press,
1710 Roe Crest Drive, North Mankato, Minnesota 56003
www.capstonepub.com

Library of Congress Cataloging-in-Publication Data
Cataloging-in-publication information is on file with the Library of Congress.
ISBN 978-1-4914-0298-6 (library binding)
ISBN 978-1-4914-0306-8 (paperback)
ISBN 978-1-4914-0302-0 (eBook PDF)

Editorial Credits
Nate LeBoutillier, editor; Juliette Peters, designer;
Eric Gohl, media researcher; Tori Abraham, production specialist

Photo Credits
Capstone Studio: Karon Dubke, 21; Library of Congress: 5, 9, 11; Newscom: akg-images/Peter Connolly, 7, Europics, 18, Everett Collection, 13; Shutterstock: 06photo, 20, Alex Mit, 1 (right), Artens, cover (bottom), Hiroshi Ichikawa, 17, njaj, 1 (left), pisaphotography, 15, Thirteen, background, Zai Aragon, cover (top)

Printed in the United States of America in North Mankato, Minnesota
032014   008087CGF14

TABLE OF CONTENTS

ON THE MOVE

Thousands of years ago, people traveled by walking or running. Those were the only choices. Over time people began riding animals and rowing boats. Then the inventions of the wheel, **steam engines**, and electric power changed everything. Today airplanes, trains, cars, and ships take travelers wherever they want to go.

· ·

steam engine—an engine that gets power by heating water to make steam

Great East River
Bridge in New York

TRANSPORTATION
IN ANCIENT TIMES

Water was important for transportation in ancient times. Many people settled near rivers and lakes. Boats and canoes that people paddled helped them **navigate** areas nearby. Large ships became the mode of transportation for Chinese, Egyptian, and Greek explorers. On land wheeled carts and dogsleds helped people travel.

navigate—to decide the direction a vehicle should travel

Ancient Greek boats

TRANSPORTATION
IN THE 1800S

The steam engine was invented in the 1700s. Years later came the first steam-driven **locomotive**. Passengers could board trains to travel from one city to another. Other steam-powered vehicles such as the car soon followed. Inventions in this era included buses, wagons, motorcycles, and even **airships**. The first bicycles with pedals also kept people moving.

● ●

locomotive—the railroad car that holds the engine to pull the train

airship—a large air balloon with engines and a place for people to ride

American trains

TRANSPORTATION
IN THE EARLY 1900S

Horseless carriages powered by gasoline motors appeared in the late 1800s, but they were expensive. Inventor Henry Ford made cars cheaper by creating **assembly lines** in 1913. Traffic jams and air **pollution** appeared as people drove farther away from home on a daily basis. Traveling wasn't just for survival or work anymore.

assembly line—an arrangement of machines and workers in a factory; work passes from one person to the next until complete

pollution—materials that hurt Earth's water, air, and land

The Model T Ford was the first affordable car in America, which made it widely popular.

Travel by air soon became a reality. **Dirigibles** were used more in the early 1900s. Wilbur and Orville Wright invented the first airplane. Their first flight in 1903 lasted 12 minutes. In 1936 American Airlines took 21 passengers to the sky.

Inventors experimented with helicopters for years before discovering rotating wings. These wings made helicopters capable of **vertical** flight.

. . . .

dirigible—an airship or blimp

vertical—straight up and down

An airplane flies
over Oakland,
California, in 1936.

TRANSPORTATION
FROM 1950-2000

Vehicles got faster and stronger after 1950. Subways, **trams**, and **trolleys** carried people to work. Airplanes and cruise ships took people on vacations. In 1969 three American astronauts circled the moon. They rode in a rocket.

FACT:
The New York City Subway has 421 stations and 842 miles (1,355 kilometers) of track. It is the largest subway system in the United States.

tram—a public transportation vehicle that moves on a special pathway

trolley—an electric street car that runs on tracks and gets power from an overhead wire

London subway

TRANSPORTATION TODAY

Transportation today is bigger and faster than ever before. In 2013 a single train company carried more than 31 million passengers in Canada and the United States. The same year people drove more than 247 million cars in the United States. Two million people fly from U.S. airports daily. More travel means improvements in comfort, safety, and speed. But scientists worry about air pollution. They are developing cleaner-running engines and power sources other than gasoline.

high-speed
Japanese train

TRANSPORTATION
IN THE FUTURE

Engineers, designers, and dreamers continue to invent new ways to travel. Future cars may not need human drivers. Trains may run only on magnetic rails. Space travel soon may include tourists. No matter the type of transportation, the **technology** will need to be safe, fast, and energy-efficient.

● ● ● ● ● ● ● ● ● ● ● ● ● ● ● ● ● ●

engineer—a person who uses science and math to plan, design, or build

technology—the use of science to do practical things

space liner designed to hold space tourists

TIMELINE

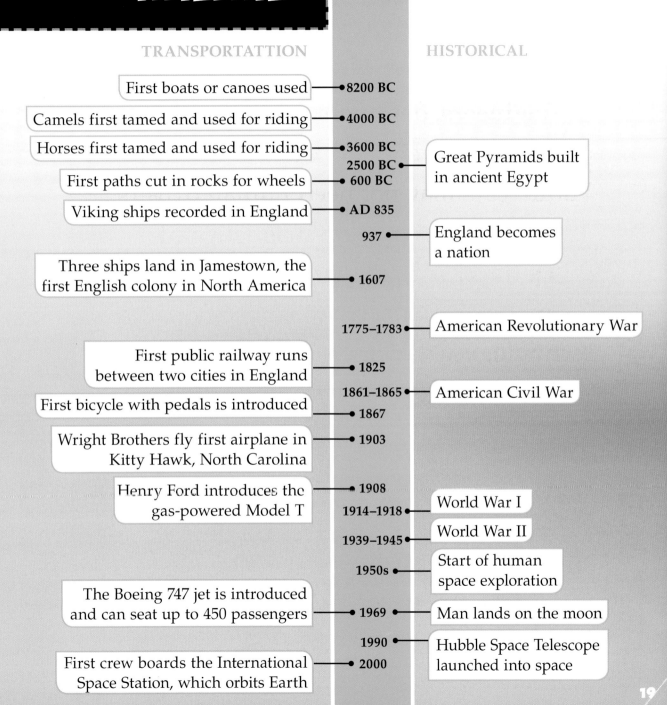

TRANSPORTATTION

HISTORICAL

First boats or canoes used	8200 BC	
Camels first tamed and used for riding	4000 BC	
Horses first tamed and used for riding	3600 BC	
	2500 BC	Great Pyramids built in ancient Egypt
First paths cut in rocks for wheels	600 BC	
Viking ships recorded in England	AD 835	
	937	England becomes a nation
Three ships land in Jamestown, the first English colony in North America	1607	
	1775–1783	American Revolutionary War
First public railway runs between two cities in England	1825	
	1861–1865	American Civil War
First bicycle with pedals is introduced	1867	
Wright Brothers fly first airplane in Kitty Hawk, North Carolina	1903	
Henry Ford introduces the gas-powered Model T	1908	
	1914–1918	World War I
	1939–1945	World War II
	1950s	Start of human space exploration
The Boeing 747 jet is introduced and can seat up to 450 passengers	1969	Man lands on the moon
	1990	Hubble Space Telescope launched into space
First crew boards the International Space Station, which orbits Earth	2000	

Fast Mover

Japan is known for its high speed "bullet" trains. These trains travel up to almost 200 miles (322 km) per hour. Engineers are now developing a magnetic levitation, or "maglev," train. It will be able to run at 310 miles (499 km) per hour, the fastest in the world. A trip from Tokyo to Nagoya that is 218 miles (351 km) should take only 40 minutes on these new trains.

Hands On:
MAKE A BOAT

What You Need:

2 empty water bottles
2 rubber bands
glue
piece of cardboard, such
  as from a cereal box
empty soup can
scissors
markers or crayons
sheet of paper
tape
straw
action figure (optional)

What You Do:

1. Remove labels from the plastic bottles. Keep caps screwed on tight.
2. Secure bottles together side by side with the rubber bands.
3. Center and glue the piece of cardboard on top of the bottles to serve as a platform.
4. Glue empty soup can to platform to serve as cabin. If desired, cut out and decorate label-sized piece of paper, and glue or tape it around can.
5. Glue straw vertically to rear of soup can. This will serve as the mast.

6. Cut out small triangle or square of paper and poke straw through paper. This will serve as the sail.
7. Place boat in bathtub, swimming pool, or open water, and set sail.
Optional: Place action figure or other small toy in the soup can to serve as the captain.

Boats were one of the first modes of transportation that allowed faraway travel.
Today cruise ships can carry 5,000 people across the world.

GLOSSARY

airship (AIR-ship)—a large air balloon with engines and a place for people to ride

assembly line (uh-SEM-blee LYN)—an arrangement of machines and workers in a factory; work passes from one person to the next until complete

dirigible (dihr-UH-juh-buhl)—an airship or blimp

engineer (en-juh-NEER)—a person who uses science and math to plan, design, or build

locomotive (lo-kuh-MOH-tiv)—the railroad car that holds the engine to pull the train

navigate (NAV-uh-gate)—to decide the direction a vehicle should travel

pollution (puh-LOO-shuhn)—materials that hurt Earth's water, air, and land

steam engine (STEEM EN-juhn)—an engine that gets power by heating water to make steam

technology (tek-NOL-uh-jee)—the use of science to do practical things

tram (TRAM)—a public transportation vehicle that moves on a special pathway

trolley (TROL-ee)—an electric street car that runs on tracks and gets power from an overhead wire

vertical (VUR-tuh-kuhl)—straight up and down

READ MORE

McGill, Jordan. *Transportation.* Community Helpers. New York: Weigl Publishers, 2012.

Rustad, Martha E. H. *Transportation in Many Cultures.* Life Around the World. Mankato, Minn.: Capstone Press, 2009.

Spengler, Kremena. *An Illustrated Timeline of Transportation.* Visual Timelines in History. Mankato, Minn.: Picture Window Books, 2012.

INTERNET SITES

FactHound offers a safe, fun way to find Internet sites related to this book. All of the sites on FactHound have been researched by our staff.

Here's all you do:

Visit *www.facthound.com*

Type in this code: 9781491402986

Check out projects, games and lots more at
www.capstonekids.com

CRITICAL THINKING USING THE COMMON CORE

1. What might have happened if people would have never invented cars, trains, and airplanes? (Integration of Knowledge and Ideas)

2. Look at the picture on page 13. How does the photo help you undertand the text on page 12? How does it help you better understand how transportation has changed over the years? (Integration of Knowledge and Ideas)

INDEX